Octopuses

by *Leighton Taylor*
photographs by *Norbert Wu*

Lerner Publications Company • Minneapolis

To the Capo Beach Research Team: Tom, Tamara, Ryland,
Cameron, Taylor, and Landon from Uncle O. —LM

To Lance, Bryan, and Thomas, with love. —NW

Additional photographs are reproduced through the courtesy of: © Bob Cranston/
www.norbertwu.com, p. 9; © Fred Bavendam, p. 18; © Jeffrey L. Rotman/CORBIS, p. 38;
© Stuart Westmorland/CORBIS, p. 39; © Stuart Westmorland/www.norbertwu.com, pp. 46–47.

Lerner Publications Company
A division of Lerner Publishing Group
241 First Avenue North
Minneapolis, MN 55401 U.S.A.

Website address: www.lernerbooks.com

Library of Congress Cataloging-in-Publication Data

Taylor, L. R. (Leighton R.)
    Octopuses / by Leighton Taylor ; photographs by Norbert Wu.
       p.   cm. — (Early bird nature books)
    Summary: Describes the anatomy, habitat, life cycle, and behavior of the various species of octopuses in oceans around the world.
    ISBN 0-8225-0068-X (lib. bdg. : alk. paper)
    1. Octopodidae—Juvenile literature. [1. Octopus.] I. Wu, Norbert, ill. II. Title. III. Series.
    QL430.3.02 T38 2003
    594'.56—dc21   2001004655

Manufactured in the United States of America
1 2 3 4 5 6 – JR – 07 06 05 04 03 02

Contents

Be a Word Detective

Can you find these words as you read about the life of the octopus? Be a detective and try to figure out what they mean. You can turn to the glossary on page 46 for help.

camouflage	mantle	stalks
coral reefs	predators	suckers
ink sac	prey	tentacles
invertebrates	siphon	yolk

Chapter 1

Octopuses can see well with their big eyes. Where do octopuses live?

Look into Its Eyes

 Whose big eyes are these? They belong to an animal who is almost all head. This animal has eight strong arms. It lives underwater. It is an octopus.

There are more than 100 species, or kinds, of octopuses. All species of octopuses live in oceans. They live in oceans all around the world. Some species live in warm water. Others live in very cold water near the North Pole or the South Pole.

All octopuses live in oceans.

A few species of octopuses live in deep water. But most live in shallow water. Some octopuses swim along coral reefs. Coral reefs are mounds of rock. The rocks in coral reefs are made by tiny ocean animals called corals.

Octopuses come in all sizes. The dwarf octopus is tiny. It is shorter than your finger. The Pacific giant octopus is huge. It is as long as a bike. Some grow to be even longer.

This octopus is a little bigger than a person's hand.

This is a Pacific giant octopus.

This octopus is upside down. It has eight tentacles.

The word *octopus* comes from the Greek word *octo. Octo* means eight. All octopuses have eight arms. One name for these arms is tentacles (TEN-tuh-kuhlz).

Octopuses are related to squids, cuttlefish, and chambered nautiluses. All these animals are invertebrates (ihn-VUR-tuh-brehts). Invertebrates are animals that have no backbones.

These divers are looking at a cuttlefish. It is related to octopuses.

Octopuses have soft bodies. The only hard part of an octopus is its beak. The beak is under its head. The beak works like jaws around an octopus's mouth.

Since an octopus is soft, it can squeeze into small places. An octopus as big as your hand can squeeze into a soda bottle.

This octopus has squeezed inside a bottle.

Octopuses do not have a backbone. But they do have a good brain.

Octopuses have big brains for their size. They can solve puzzles and open locks. They are amazing animals.

Chapter 2

An octopus eats fish. What else does an octopus eat?

Octopus Hunters

All octopuses are predators (PREH-duh-turz). Predators are animals that hunt and eat other animals. Octopuses hunt and eat small ocean animals like fish, crabs, and clams. The animals an octopus hunts are called its prey.

This octopus is hiding in some rocks.

Sometimes an octopus just waits for its prey to come along. The octopus hides in a crack or a cave.

But sometimes an octopus stalks its prey. To stalk prey, an octopus crawls along slowly. It crawls over rocks. It looks for prey. Octopuses can see well, even in dim light. Many octopuses hunt in the dark.

Sometimes an octopus looks for food on the bottom of the ocean.

This octopus is feeling for food with its tentacles.

The suckers on the bottom of this octopus's tentacles help it feel prey.

An octopus also uses its tentacles to hunt. It feels around in places where it cannot see. Its tentacles are covered with small, round suckers. The suckers can taste and feel prey.

17

When an octopus finds prey, it grabs the prey with its tentacles. The octopus uses its tentacles to move the prey to its mouth. An octopus's mouth is hard to see. It is hidden by a layer of muscle that covers most of the octopus. This layer of muscle is called the mantle.

This octopus is eating a crab.

Crabs have hard shells. Octopuses use their beak to crush a crab's hard shell.

Some prey, like crabs, have hard shells. An octopus uses its beak to crush a crab's shell. It can also use its beak to drill a hole in the shell. It sucks on the hole to suck out the meat.

This octopus is not poisonous.

Some octopuses make a kind of poison. The poison is in their saliva, or spit. To poison prey, an octopus cuts the prey with its beak. The poison flows into the cut. Then the prey cannot move.

Most octopuses cannot harm people. But some species can. The blue-ringed octopus lives in the ocean near Australia. It is tiny. But its poison can kill large prey. It can even kill people.

The blue-ringed octopus makes a deadly poison.

Chapter 3

This picture shows an octopus hiding. Where do octopuses hide?

Hiding

Do you eat octopuses? Some people do. Some sharks, seals, and other predators also eat octopuses.

To stay away from predators, an octopus hides. It squeezes under a rock. It scoots into an empty shell. Or it wiggles into a bottle.

An octopus hides in many places. This octopus is hiding on the bottom of the ocean.

An octopus also has other ways to hide. It can make itself look like the things around it. Then predators cannot see it. This way of hiding is called camouflage (KAM-uh-flahzh).

Changing color is a good way for an octopus to hide.

This tiny octopus is changing color as it crawls along.

To camouflage itself, an octopus changes color. When the octopus crawls on white sand, it turns white. When it climbs on gray rocks, it turns gray.

Some octopuses can also make themselves look smooth or bumpy. They can even look shaggy. An octopus can look like a bumpy gray rock covered with shaggy seaweed.

An octopus can make itself look bumpy. This bumpy octopus is very hard to see.

This octopus blends in with the sand.

This is a reef shark. Reef sharks sometimes eat octopuses.

Sometimes a predator does see an octopus. The octopus has to get away fast. So it shoots out a jet of water. The water comes from a tube behind the octopus's eye. This tube is called a siphon (SYE-fuhn). When water shoots out of the siphon, the octopus jets ahead.

This octopus is
jetting through
the water.

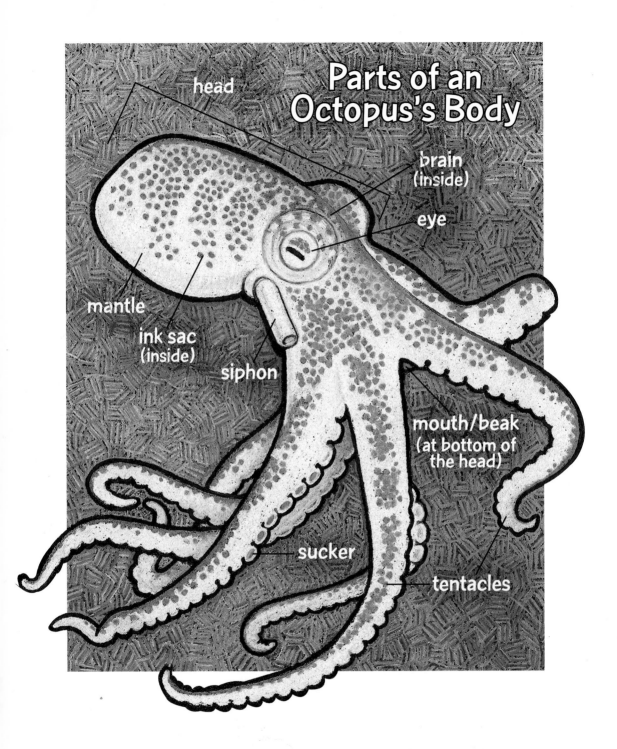

Parts of an Octopus's Body

head

brain
(inside)

eye

mantle

ink sac
(inside)

siphon

mouth/beak
(at bottom of
the head)

sucker

tentacles

Some octopuses can shoot a jet of black ink out of their body. The ink comes from the octopus's ink sac. The ink sac is a bag inside an octopus's body. It is full of ink. When the ink shoots out, it makes a black cloud. The cloud fools predators. A predator thinks the octopus is hiding in the cloud. Meanwhile, the octopus swims away.

This stream of black ink is coming from the octopus. The ink is not the same as the ink in a pen.

Chapter 4

These are octopus eggs. Where does a mother octopus lay her eggs?

Babies with Eight Arms

 An octopus starts life as an egg. An octopus egg is soft and white.

A mother octopus lays many eggs at one time. She lays them in a bunch. A bunch of octopus eggs looks like a bunch of white grapes. Each egg has a baby octopus inside.

The mother lays her eggs where predators cannot find them. She lays them in a cave. Or she lays them under a rock.

A mother octopus chooses a hidden place to lay eggs.

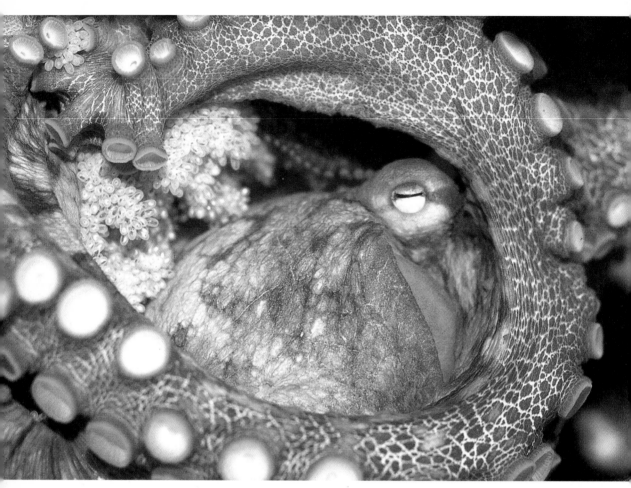

This mother octopus is wrapping her tentacles around her eggs.

After a mother octopus lays her eggs, she stays near them. She curls her tentacles around them. She uses camouflage to look like a big rock. Then predators and other animals stay away.

Each octopus egg has a yolk. The yolk is food for the baby inside the egg.

In a few weeks, the baby hatches from the egg. A baby octopus is tiny when it hatches. It is so small it could sit on your thumb. It looks like a tiny adult octopus.

Each octopus egg has a tiny baby inside (left). *This baby octopus has hatched from an egg* (right).

Baby octopuses can take care of themselves.

The mother octopus dies after the eggs hatch. All octopus babies take care of themselves. They know how to hide from predators. They know how to hunt.

The babies of some species live on the ocean bottom. They hunt and eat small ocean animals like tiny crabs and worms. The babies of other species float along in the open sea. They eat tiny animals that float by.

A baby octopus grows up in about one year.

Baby octopuses grow fast. In about one year, a baby octopus will be as big as an adult. Then it will have babies of its own.

Chapter 5

This diver is meeting an octopus underwater. How long have people known about octopuses?

People and Octopuses

 People have known about octopuses for thousands of years. All that time, people have eaten octopuses.

People have studied octopuses, too. About 2,300 years ago, a famous scientist named Aristotle lived in Greece. He studied octopuses. Then he wrote about them. He knew that octopuses can see well. He knew that octopuses are smart.

People learn about octopuses by watching what they do.

These tiny octopuses are in an aquarium. A scientist is using tweezers to move one of the octopuses.

Modern scientists are testing octopuses. They know that octopuses can tell different shapes apart. Scientists test this by putting balls, dice, and other shapes near an octopus. The octopus gets a treat if it grabs a certain shape. It does not get a treat if it grabs the other shapes.

The octopus learns to grab the right shape. It remembers the right shape for several weeks. This shows that octopuses learn well.

Scientists are learning a lot from octopuses. They are learning how a brain works. This helps us to understand people better.

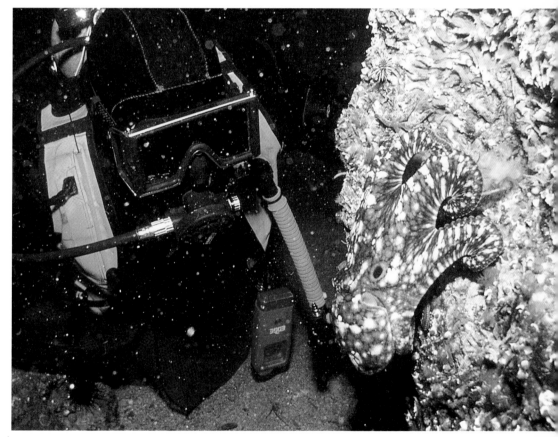

Scientists know that octopuses learn quickly.

Do you want to meet an octopus? You can see one at a zoo or an aquarium. You may see one at the seashore. Who knows what will happen if you look into an octopus's eyes? Maybe it will learn from you, too.

You can learn a lot by meeting an octopus face to face.

Maybe octopuses learn from people, too.

On Sharing a Book

As you know, adults greatly influence a child's attitude toward reading. When a child sees you read, or when you share a book with a child, you're sending a message that reading is important. Show the child that reading a book together is important to you. Find a comfortable, quiet place. Turn off the television and limit other distractions, such as telephone calls.

Be prepared to start slowly. Take turns reading parts of this book. Stop and talk about what you're reading. Talk about the photographs. You may find that much of the shared time is spent discussing just a few pages. This discussion time is valuable for both of you, so don't move through the book too quickly. If the child begins to lose interest, stop reading. Continue sharing the book at another time. When you do pick up the book again, be sure to revisit the parts you have already read. Most importantly, enjoy the book!

Be a Vocabulary Detective

You will find a word list on page 5. Words selected for this list are important to the understanding of the topic of this book. Encourage the child to be a word detective and search for the words as you read the book together. Talk about what the words mean and how they are used in the sentence. Do any of these words have more than one meaning? You will find these words defined in a glossary on page 46.

What about Questions?

Use questions to make sure the child understands the information in this book. Here are some suggestions:

> What did this paragraph tell us? What does this picture show? What do you think we'll learn about next? Could an octopus live near you? Why/Why not? How far would you have to travel to see an octopus? What do octopuses eat? How does a mother octopus take care of her eggs? How do octopuses stay safe from other animals? Are octopuses like people? How are they the same/different? What is your favorite part of the book? Why? Did any part of the book surprise you?

If the child has questions, don't hesitate to respond with questions of your own such as: What do *you* think? Why? What is it that you don't know? If the child can't remember certain facts, turn to the index.

Introducing the Index

The index is an important learning tool. It helps readers get information quickly without searching throughout the whole book. Turn to the index on page 47. Choose an entry, such as *hiding,* and ask the child to use the index to find out how an octopus hides. Repeat this exercise with as many entries as you like. Ask the child to point out the differences between an index and a glossary. (The index helps readers find information quickly, while the glossary tells readers what words mean.)

All the World in Metric!

Although our monetary system is in metric units (based on multiples of 10), the United States is one of the few countries in the world that does not use the metric system of measurement. Here are some conversion activities you and the child can do using a calculator:

WHEN YOU KNOW:	MULTIPLY BY:	TO FIND:
miles	1.609	kilometers
feet	0.3048	meters
inches	2.54	centimeters
gallons	3.787	liters
tons	0.907	metric tons
pounds	0.454	kilograms

Activities

Try making a four-headed octopus. First, find three friends who are about as tall as you are. Get as close as you can to each other. Stand still. Then have everyone raise their arms. Together, you have eight arms. Try passing a ball from hand to hand. Is it hard or easy? Try clapping your hand against someone else's hand. Is it easier for an octopus to use eight arms than for you and your friends to use eight arms? Do you know why/why not?

Find out how an octopus holds on with the suckers on its tentacles. Take a rubber suction cup like a toilet plunger. Press it against a smooth floor. This pushes all the air out from the suction cup. Can you feel the cup sticking to the floor? What would happen if you had suction cups on your hands?

Glossary

camouflage (KAM-uh-flahzh): patterns and colors that cover an animal and make the animal hard to see

coral reefs: mounds of rock made by tiny sea animals called corals

ink sac: the bag inside an octopus that makes a black, inky liquid

invertebrates (ihn-VUR-tuh-brehts): all of the animals without backbones

mantle: the layer of muscle that covers most of an octopus

predators (PREH-duh-turz): animals who hunt and eat other animals

prey: animals who are hunted and eaten by other animals

siphon (SYE-fuhn): the tube an octopus uses to shoot out water

stalks: hunts animals by sneaking up on them

suckers: round cups on the bottom of an octopus's tentacles. Suckers help an octopus feel, taste, smell, and hold on to things.

tentacles (TEN-tuh-kuhlz): the eight arms of an octopus

yolk: the ball of food inside an egg that feeds the baby growing in the egg

Index

About the Author

Leighton Taylor is a marine biologist who began studying the sea while fishing as a small boy in California. He went to graduate school in Hawaii. Hawaii's warm water, bright fish, and coral reefs convinced him to spend his life studying and writing about the animals who live in the sea. He earned a Ph.D. degree at Scripps Institution of Oceanography. He loves to dive and has made many expeditions in the Pacific Ocean, the Indian Ocean, and the Caribbean Sea. He has discovered and named several new species of sharks, including the deep-sea Megamouth shark.

About the Photographer

Norbert Wu is an independent photographer and filmmaker who specializes in marine issues. The author and photographer of several books on wildlife and photography, he has assembled a photographic library of marine wildlife that is one of the most comprehensive in the world. His recent films include a high-definition television (HDTV) program on Antarctica's underwater world for WNET/Thirteen New York's *Nature* series that airs on PBS. He has been awarded several National Science Foundation (NSF) Artists and Writers Grants to document Antarctica's underwater world and a Pew Marine Conservation Fellowship.